What Our Readers Have Said...

Applicability

"These books are great tools that should be used as guidelines for our everyday supervisory practices. You need to take the time to do a short self-evaluation when reading them."

•

"The Pinpoint Training Series delivers information that could be used in a lot different areas."

•

"The things and problems we deal with everyday are discussed in these books."

Convenience

"I like this because I can take them with me to read at a convenient time. I feel the little time I have to spend in the office is best use on activities that directly relate to revenue opportunities. I like the short amount of time it takes to keep up with these."

•

"I prefer the self-study approach; it fits in with my schedule."

•

"I like the fact that the format allows the books to be reviewed as time permits. All work has been conducted on personal, evening/weekend time."

•

"Easy to use... if you put the time into it."

Challenge

"My thought is that the real value of these books comes into effect when doing the action plans."

•

"I like the fact that the format allows assignments to be reviewed as time permits."

Clarity

"Short and sweet. These books are easy to comprehend."

•

"Easy to use, understand, and reference if needed."

Relevance

"I have enjoyed reading these books. They are relevant to today's work environment and the ongoing change in the way we manage our workforce."

•

"I believe the contents of the Pinpoint series are excellent. It causes one to reflect on the daily dynamics in working with oneself as well as with management and peers."

Facilitating Change

Pinpoint Leadership Skill Development Training Series

TIMOTHY F. BEDNARZ

MAJORIUM
BUSINESS PRESS

Pinpoint Leadership Skill Development Training Series
"Facilitating Change"
Timothy F. Bednarz

Graphic design: Monika Pawlak

Majorium Business Press
2025 Main Street
Stevens Point, WI 54481
715.342.1018 • 800.654.4935

ISBN 978-1-882181-58-2

Printed in the United States of America

Introduction

The Pinpoint Leadership Skill Development Training Series is designed for targeted training and education regarding increased improvement in a specific skill or competency.

Each book within this series is designed to be easy to use, understand and apply to your job. It can be used as a basis for training individuals, as a discussion guide or as a personal training tool.

Each chapter within this book discusses a specific concept. When you have completed all eight chapters you should have a 360° perspective of the topic.

Additionally, each chapter is divided into specific sections:

- The first section provides you with an overview of the topic
- The Implications section discusses why the concept is important, and why it is important to learn and apply.
- The Strategies, Tips & Techniques to Apply section teaches how to use and apply the particular concept to your work.
- The Points to Ponder section gives you something to think about or to be discussed with a group setting. These are questions not meant to be immediately answered, but to be pondered over time.
- The Training Activity section provides you with the tools to transfer what you have learned to your job. It is designed to help create an action plan to effectively apply the concept.

Each of the topics in this series is time-tested and proven in the marketplace. They have been used by thousands of employees as training tools. Many of the users have commented that what made these books valuable, was the ability to refer to them when a problem surfaced. They indicated that they remembered reading about the exact problem. They referred back to these books and found an appropriate solution.

You will find them equally valuable as a resource in your professional development library.

Table of Contents

LEARNING OBJECTIVES:

- To identify and apply the elements, factors and principles that define organizational change.
- To identify the implications and ramifications of change and its impact.
- To overcome problems and pitfalls related to embracing and implementing change.
- To identify and analyze the various impacts and effects change has upon organizational and leadership decision making.
- To apply effective strategies to implement and embrace change within an organization.

Why Change Is Inevitable

For decades, many U.S. companies worked within a relatively stable environment, isolated from world competition through the late 1970s as many foreign competitors rebuilt from the devastation of World War II. Dominating world markets for approximately 20 years after the conclusion of the war, many U.S. companies developed a false sense of security. With foreign competition becoming more formidable in the late 1970s and into the early 80s, the pace of change has become unrelenting.

Leaders must comes to grips with the concept of change in the marketplace and learn to see change as an ally to be welcomed rather than an enemy to be feared. The lessons of the 80s and 90s have shown that change is a reality in the marketplace fueled by a number of factors that are not going away. If anything, change will be taking place at an increasingly frenetic pace. Leaders must use its impetus as a positive force within their organization.

IMPLICATIONS — WHAT THIS MEANS TO YOU

Change presents leaders with the opportunity to rise up to meet the challenges coming to their organization. It is a leader's flexibility that allows them to anticipate, adapt to and facilitate change within their organizations.

Leaders should be aware that times of change and turmoil have produced some of the most recognizable leaders in recent American history: Rockefeller, Carnegie and Morgan of the Industrial Age and Gates of the Information Revolution, all of whom turned adversity into opportunity. This is the challenge change brings to today's leader.

STRATEGIES, TIPS & TECHNIQUES TO APPLY

Leaders must come to grips with the inevitability of change in the marketplace and understand what is fueling its ever-increasing pace. Rather than fear change, leaders should use their personal vision to lead their organization through times of instability and uncertainty.

The factors fueling change and requiring serious consideration by leaders include:

Economic Uncertainty

The events of September 11, 2001, and the associated slowdown of the U.S. economy highlight the economic uncertainty every organization faces.

The globalization of business and rise of electronic communications in the closing decades of the 20th century have made all companies more vulnerable to international economic events spawned by terrorism, the instability of oil supply and prices, and the close proximity and interconnectivity of world economies. These have been intensified by an increase in global mergers and acquisitions, instability of world currency exchange rates, and the record number of business startups and failures, all of which fuel economic uncertainty and demand an organization's response to rapidly changing conditions.

This environment calls for leaders who look out beyond current events and anticipate overall shifts and trends in the world economy. These shifts must be translated into the specific impact they will have on their organization, strategy and action.

Technology

The introduction of the microchip has fueled changes in technology at a pace never before seen. Faster and more sophisticated computer designs and software have made for innovations allowing companies to reduce design cycles and respond more quickly to customer preferences and demands. The ability of customers to interact electronically with their suppliers gives them more power and control over the manufacturing process while reducing the overall costs of production. This has impacted not only the design-to-manufacture cycle, but also an organization's ability to develop smaller and more flexible production facilities to better produce and meet changing customer demands.

Competition

Technology has also spawned new competitors creating a host of "me-too" products reducing the space that often differentiated one competitor from another. Technology has also increased competition not only from the developing world but from the newly industrialized countries of South Korea, China, and countries in South America and the Pacific Rim.

Additional competition is being created by technology in the form of entrepreneurial companies targeting profitable niche markets. These are chipping away at many of the advantages once held by manufacturing stalwarts. The lower cost of new technology has allowed these companies to enter and successfully compete in markets heretofore considered untouchable.

The power of the Internet has increased the reach of virtually every competitor to the entire world market. Where in the past it was expensive to expand markets, the Internet has now given any customer a wealth of choices when choosing a supplier.

Consumer Tastes

The pace of change has impacted consumer tastes due to the proliferation of options and information. People are also increasingly affluent and sophisticated, demanding higher quality products and services with a host of options. The continuing, Internet-fueled information explosion promises to increase these demands.

The results of these factors include continued uncertainty and a closer aligning of both companies and economies.

Technology will cause the demise of mass production in many industries as more efficient applications make reduced economies of scale more feasible. This will provide customers with more product options and increased market fragmentation as companies target more profitable niche markets for their products or services. This will result in a demand for high quality products and services produced more quickly in response to market demands.

The overall outcome is a more complex environment for leaders to work within, understand and to lead their organizations through. This will increase demands for more flexible and results-oriented leaders as change continues.

Potential Results

The future for leaders is not as dismal as one might think. The visionary leader can expect to see more niche-oriented market opportunities featuring shorter production runs. If their organization has not already flattened many of its levels of bureaucracies, this will inevitably happen as the business is reshaped to be more responsive and adaptive to the market.

The challenge for the leader is to create a more quality-conscious organization that demands the workforce's participation in overcoming the problems and issues change will bring. The trend of the organization dealing with ongoing change will be in the development of adding value through their biggest asset—their employees.

POINTS TO PONDER — SOMETHING TO THINK ABOUT

1. Do you fear or embrace the opportunities change brings to your organization?
2. What personal ideas, perceptions, beliefs or attitudes do you need to alter about change and the challenges it generates?

TRAINING ACTIVITY — APPLICATION & ACTION PLAN

Take time to look beyond the horizon and examine some of the bigger issues and trends impacting your industry and company.

1. Select two or three major issues you see affecting your company in the next several years.
2. Examine each of these issues closely.
3. Determine how each will specifically impact your company and the department, unit or division you lead.
4. Pinpoint the opportunities each presents.
5. Identify strategies that can be implemented to take advantage of various emerging opportunities.
6. Discuss these observations with your superiors.
7. Develop an action plan to implement your strategies.

2

Change Equates to Opportunity

Customers, competition and technology compel every organization to adapt to change. The success and speed of change is dependent upon several key factors closely associated with leadership. Institutionalized management practices and structures can create formidable obstacles to internal change that prevent organizations from taking advantage of opportunities presenting themselves in short windows of time. These obstacles present a challenge to all leaders in the organization.

In most organizations individuals are taught to manage, not to lead. However, within these organizational cultures management is often equated with leadership. This is a common fallacy that often prevents organizations from effecting change and taking advantage of the opportunities it affords.

Management is a precise set of processes that keeps a complicated system of people, resources and technology running smoothly. The management process includes planning, budgeting, organizing, controlling and other like functions.

Leadership, on the other hand, is a set of processes that initially creates the organization and allows it to adapt to a variety of changing circumstances.

IMPLICATIONS – WHAT THIS MEANS TO YOU

This distinction is important for leaders to understand because leadership defines the future for the organization, aligns people with the vision and motivates them to make it happen despite obstacles along the way. It is important to make the distinction between management and leadership because transforming an organization in the face of change requires a majority of leadership skills and a minority of management skills. While management was required to build and staff the large corporate organizations of the past, leadership is required to transform them in the face of change for the future.

STRATEGIES, TIPS & TECHNIQUES TO APPLY

The key factors of change within any organization are all leadership rather than management-based. In the past, management was essential to internally build and maintain large organizations and bureaucracies. While management is still important, organizations faced with rapidly changing technologies, markets and competition must focus their efforts *externally* to effectively handle change and take advantage of the opportunities that change presents to them. This external focus requires the key factors of leadership.

The reasons for an external focus are straightforward. Internally focused managers and employees tend to be myopic in their thinking, which makes it difficult to identify the external forces presenting both threats and opportunities to the organization.

Insular thinking is designed to protect internal bureaucracies and political power bases, and denies the existence of the forces of change buffeting the organization. Since they deny the forces of change, these individuals are highly resistant and build internal obstacles to it within the organization. This rigid thinking represents a formidable barrier for leaders to overcome.

Before leaders can emerge and challenge these internal barriers, they must understand how the key factors of change compare to the traditional management structure and how leadership and management vary in both their style and approach to change. While management can support leadership in the accomplishment of goals and objectives, most organizational cultures have a reversed environment where management dictates what leadership should and can do.

The following comparisons are where many of the management/leadership conflicts occur with management imposing its principles upon and constraining leadership.

Planning and Budgeting vs. Establishing Direction

The role of management is to establish detailed steps and schedules that control and direct the organization toward the accomplishment of its goals and objectives. Individuals and organizational resources are allotted according to need and assigned to specific tasks.

The role of leadership is to develop and define an organizational vision for the future. Along with their vision, leaders develop strategies to produce the necessary changes required to achieve their vision.

The conflict in established organizations run by managers is that they wish to have leaders work within the constraints of established plans and budgets. This limits and confines the leader's ability to act and effect overall change.

Rather, planning and budgeting should be used to support the leader's goals and vision to implement necessary organizational change. This presents a challenge for leaders, as they have to effect internal change before they can achieve external change.

Organizing and Staffing vs. Aligning People

The conflict between organizing and staffing versus the alignment of people is an argument of form over function. Many entrenched managers have institutionalized several management functions creating highly structured programs that assist the organization in achieving its institutionalized goals and objectives. These include policies, procedures, methods and systems to control and direct the employees and resources of the organization.

While leaders understand the validity of a management structure and the need for it to support a leader's vision, goals and objectives, they are first guided by the principles of aligning people with their vision. This is accomplished by communicating direction in words and deeds to everyone whose cooperation is needed to influence the creation of teams and coalitions that understand and accept the vision.

Once teams and coalitions are internally established, leaders can use the management functions of organizing and staffing to support these efforts, rather than be constrained by them.

Controlling and Problem Solving vs. Motivating and Inspiring

The use of control methods and techniques is management's way to monitor results and identify deviations from the plan. Problem solving techniques are instituted to use organizational resources to resolve issues.

The leader will use these methods and techniques only after motivating and inspiring people to overcome the major internal and external barriers to change. The fundamental difference lies in management using methods to implement solutions, while leaders motivate people to change.

Predictability and Order vs. Change and Opportunity

The fundamental difference between management and leadership is in the final results. Management focuses on the short-term results expected by various stakeholders in the organization such as meeting budgets and quotas and producing an adequate ROI. If this is the only focus—predictability, order and short-term results—the ability of the organization to adapt and meet the forces of change is greatly inhibited.

The focus of leadership is driving the organization through change as defined by their vision. While this may impact the organization's short-term goals, it has the potential of producing extremely useful change, taking advantage of emerging opportunities and beneficially transforming the organization. This results in new products, services, approaches and methods positively impacting the organization over the long run.

POINTS TO PONDER — SOMETHING TO THINK ABOUT

1. How standardized are the internal management methods and practices in your organization?
2. Do you see external forces of change impacting their efficacy?

TRAINING ACTIVITY — APPLICATION & ACTION PLAN

1. Identify the internal barriers to change you face by addressing the following areas of conflict:
    - Planning and budgeting vs. establishing direction
    - Organizing and staffing vs. aligning people
    - Controlling and problem solving vs. motivating and inspiring
    - Predictability and order vs. change and opportunity
2. Determine the actions you need to take to overcome any existing barriers.
3. Identify other leaders that are experiencing similar problems. Align yourself with them to establish a coalition.
4. Brainstorm ideas and strategies to overcome the specific internal barriers you identified.

3

Anticipating and Handling Employee Fears of Change

Before leaders can successfully lead their organizational units through a transformational change, they must overcome existing general fears and negative attitudes. Most of these fears and attitudes have been formed over the past two decades by actions and decisions organizations have made that have detrimentally affected individual employees.

From the 1980s on, businesses have faced the greatest overall restructuring since the Industrial Revolution. The depth and scope of this restructuring has been painful. Many employees have experienced downsizing, layoffs and a host of management fads, including the chaos, uncertainty and heightened frustration of reengineering. The methods used often resulted in covering and masking a number of management actions and mistakes.

Pain was further increased by the visible unfairness and callousness of many employee layoffs. The result left for leaders to deal with is an employee mindset that translates into a lack of willingness to contribute personal initiative and productive work. This reflects itself in less effective teaming efforts and a lower output of quality decisions and products, as well as decreasing the loyalty leaders require from their unit members to lead their organization through the ongoing transformational process.

IMPLICATIONS — WHAT THIS MEANS TO YOU

This is important for leaders to grasp because organizations competing in the 21st century need the willing help and assistance of intelligent, motivated, collaborative and enterprising employees. This presents leaders with a real challenge: they must first work with their employees to overcome the problems and sentiments of past organizational actions before moving forward into an active transformation. Organizational stakeholders and investors who want to see increased results and overall improvement further complicate the process.

STRATEGIES, TIPS & TECHNIQUES TO APPLY

The International Survey Research Corporation, which tracks employee satisfaction for Fortune 1000 companies, reported that since 1989 employees:

- Feel that management fails to provide clear direction.
- Do not believe what management says.
- Are less sure about keeping their jobs.
- Worry about their company's future.
- Fear being laid off.
- Feel overall morale is lower.

These facts frame the starting point defining where many leaders find themselves in the face of transformational change in their organizations. While time heals all wounds, most leaders do not have this luxury in the face of the chaotic events and issues.

The most practical answer to overcoming these fears and attitudes is increasing employee empowerment. However, this is not likely to work without the total overall commitment of everyone holding a leadership position. Leadership can come from the ranks of senior managers or from organizational unit and team leaders. Any major transition will not work without a commitment from each one.

In addition to employee empowerment, leaders need to establish working teams to tackle ongoing problems and concerns. It is better to establish multiple teams than to create one involving every employee in the organizational unit; the best workable size is between five and six members. In many instances, teams can work on the same problems. This furnishes a method of developing multiple solutions and alternatives. A collaborative team can be established to select the best solution and then assign specific aspects of it to each team to address and implement.

Employing a team approach demands specific leadership skills, including:

- Goal setting
- Planning
- Effective follow-up procedures

If leaders fail to develop one of these three skills or eliminate them from their leadership contributions, the team will break down.

Leaders furthermore cannot assume that if they simply form a team, participants will decipher what needs to be done and how things need to be accomplished. Leaders must train unit members in working together in teams, focusing on the important issues, dealing with other teammates, and getting results.

In order for this training to be successful, leaders must make sure the following team elements are adhered to, including:

- Clarity of goals
- Good communication
- Effective dissemination of business objectives so the team understands how it fits into the general business plan
- An effective process to guide and direct the actions of the team

While empowerment and an effective team approach will not immediately resolve many of the nagging employee problems and attitudes a leader must actively deal with, it does establish a foundation for improved performance and participation. As leaders initially start the process, they will need to develop strategies to cope with and address the emotional baggage issues brought to the table by their employees. They must allow the venting of frustrations and criticisms, then eliminate each of these issues in turn until full participation is achieved.

POINTS TO PONDER — SOMETHING TO THINK ABOUT

1. Have you seen a deterioration in employee attitudes due to past management decisions and actions?
2. What do you see as the biggest challenge in overcoming these negative employee attitudes?

TRAINING ACTIVITY — APPLICATION & ACTION PLAN

Perform a skills assessment on your own leadership abilities:

1. Review the following three areas:
    a. Goal setting
    b. Planning
    c. Effective follow up procedures
2. Identify particular strengths and weaknesses in each of these skill areas.
3. Determine the actions needed to strengthen your weaker skill areas.

4

The Implications of Organizational Change

As the structure and focus of the organization evolves in the face of change, the importance of overall leadership throughout the entire organization is elevated. While rigid management policies cannot readily adapt to a changing environment, the principles of leadership are well-suited to these situations.

One of the challenges of leadership lies in the evolving role of the leader. Many have been trained and are well-practiced in management and bureaucratic principles. Yet, it is the leader that must change and evolve before they can lead their organization through a transformational change. In this capacity, like it or not, the leadership role is thrust upon them.

IMPLICATIONS — WHAT THIS MEANS TO YOU

It is important to understand the implications of organizational change because circumstances often dictate the leader's roles and actions. While reluctant at first to be thrust into the role of leader, they often learn that many individuals look to them and depend upon their direction in difficult changing times. It is this difficulty and stress a leader must face that polishes and hones their skills and enables them to perform at their peak. True leaders at every level will rise to meet the personal challenges presented to them, while others will shrink from their responsibilities.

STRATEGIES, TIPS & TECHNIQUES TO APPLY

Change and the transformation that is produced within the organization have ramifications and implications to leaders. Their individual roles and responsibilities are elevated as the organization shifts its direction. These implications often include:

Focus

Leaders must shift the organization's focus from internal procedures and methods stressing efficiency and productivity outwardly toward meeting the needs of their customers. This is one of the most dramatic changes most organizations face as they adapt themselves to compete within the global marketplace. While issues such as efficiency, quality and productivity still have major roles within any organization, these are also focused around how an organization can best serve the customer rather than itself.

The role of the leader in this shift in focus is to make sure that all individuals under his or her direction also shift their own focus. Teams and workgroups are designed around the principles of how a product or service can be delivered more effectively and efficiently to the customer while improving and sustaining overall quality. Only when leaders can communicate and lead their employees toward this goal can this shift be successfully accomplished.

Structure

The role of the leader in a changing environment is to also adapt the structure of the organization to match the external focus. This means a decentralization of authority replaced by a culture of empowerment. In this capacity, the role of the leader is to lead rather than manage. The role of employees is to manage. This means creating performance information systems that provides employees with specific data, most often focused on the customer. This sharing of information provides the empowered employee with the information he or she needs to make qualified decisions to manage their responsibilities.

In this environment the leader is responsible for training their employees to work effectively together as a team toward the accomplishment of their externally focused goals. The leader is also responsible for freeing their employees of complicated internal interdependencies that characterize a bureaucratic structure, which allows them to better serve the needs of the customer.

Decision Making

When leaders free empowered employees of bureaucratic structures, enable the free-flow of information and train them to work in teams focused on the needs of the customer, they also free them and the organization to make more critical and timely decisions more quickly. This is especially true when decisions are based on meeting the customer's needs rather than those of the organization. Internal politics and personal agendas are pushed aside to focus on the quality of the product and what the customer wants.

Culture

As the organizational environment transforms itself, leaders must develop a more open and candid culture free of internal politics and personal agendas. This can present leaders with a challenge, as those individuals most deeply entrenched in the old structure have the most to lose and are most resistant to change.

Many employees who possess valuable knowledge in production and operational techniques and methods often known as "native knowledge" are reluctant to share this information out of fear that it will be used against them, that it is their "bargaining chip" to keep their jobs. Many are reluctant to share their expertise with a company they do not trust due to past policies and actions. Yet it is this precise expertise that leaders must uncover and utilize in the team environment if the organization is to excel in delivering superior products and service for their customers.

These are the challenges leaders must face and overcome as they build trust and rapport with their employees.

Risk

As organizations transform themselves in the face of change, most become more risk-tolerant as new ideas evolve from empowered employees and teams and are implemented. Decision making is decentralized from the leaders and diversified to the employees and teams now responsible for managing under the leader's direction. Since decisions are made at lower levels, all in the organization share the risks.

Additionally, when decisions are focused on the customer, not internally on operations and productions, risks are actually lowered because decisions are based upon customer demands and needs.

POINTS TO PONDER — SOMETHING TO THINK ABOUT

1. Does the thought of change within your organization frighten you, or do you embrace it?
2. How do you think you can best serve the needs of your customers? What defines your personal contribution?

TRAINING ACTIVITY — APPLICATION & ACTION PLAN

Leaders can be found at all levels within an organization. Taking into account your position in the organization, identify the specific implications and changes you see within your area of leadership responsibility as you examine the following factors:

- Focus
- Structure
- Decision making
- Culture

- Risk

As you review these areas, remember that leaders have a vision. Identify how these factors define your vision of where you feel the organization should be going.

5

A Leader's Response to Change

It is difficult to predict leaders' responses to change, as they must continually be on guard for unpredictable occurrences and forces, and in some cases immediately respond to a series of unknown and unanticipated events and circumstances. The only certainty is that change will occur, and leaders must be at the forefront of the process regardless of circumstances and apprehensions.

Change undoubtedly poses a challenge to every leader. This is because it can be anticipated only to the degree that it is predictable. Long-term changes and trends can be generally anticipated, but these changes are often complicated by numerous factors and elements continually altering and transforming themselves at varying rates of speed.

The total process is like trying to navigate across a table filled with a number of spinning tops: each spins at different directions and speeds, bumping into one another, knocking each other out of their orbits. Controlling the process of change is similar. In this type of atmosphere it is extremely difficult, and at times virtually impossible, to plot a straight and stable course.

IMPLICATIONS — WHAT THIS MEANS TO YOU

The difficulty in controlling the process of change is important for leaders to appreciate as their reaction demands a high degree of flexibility and adaptability to rapidly altering environments, circumstances and events. Their response must include continual and active involvement in the midst of change, "getting their hands dirty" as problems and crises erupt, handling and resolving each as the process of transformation moves through its charted course.

STRATEGIES, TIPS & TECHNIQUES TO APPLY

The concept of change also demands that leaders embrace stability and instability within the organization as it transforms itself. Several strategies that leaders need to employ during periods of change include:

Being Visible

The very nature of leadership demands that leaders be actively involved in their organizational unit. Leadership does not emanate from behind a desk or within an office. Leaders must be active and visible in the front lines of their business. Only when leaders are out and about among their employees can they see and feel the pace of progress, and witness firsthand the problems their employees are encountering.

Testing

Paces of change and organizational transformations demand that countless ideas be constantly generated and experimented with at all levels. Undoubtedly, some ideas will fail and some will succeed. The only way leaders can sort out the winners from the losers is by constantly applying new ideas and concepts on the line to test for feasibility and adaptability to their organization.

Listening

As leaders become increasingly visible, it is important that they simultaneously begin to develop listening forums where everyone within their organizational unit is sharing new ideas, celebrating minor successes and learning from small failures. This increases the synergy between employees, builds and solidifies team bonds, and enhances overall organizational cohesiveness.

Appreciating Failure

As aforementioned, an organization's response to change as it transforms itself implies countless new ideas and concepts are being experimented with on a regular basis. Leaders know that constant experimentation means that they must test concepts, ideas and strategies rapidly—fail or succeed fast—and adjust quickly.

Active leaders must immediately discard bad ideas and learn from their failures. However, no idea can be deemed good or bad unless it has been adequately tested. The key is to learn from the failures and quickly move on to the next idea, building knowledge and expertise from a continual string of ineffective results, failures and shortcomings.

Taking Action

Leaders in the fast pace of change must be proactive rather than reactive. They cannot let the organizational bureaucracy interfere with the progress of their organizational unit. At times they must actively work against this bureaucracy when it regulates or inhibits the testing and experimentation of new ideas and concepts.

Effective leaders do not only involve their frontline employees in concept, idea and method experimentation, they encourage the participation of multi-functional teams as well, and work to get them fully involved in the process.

Learning from Customers

Leaders have learned that the external influence of the customer is a stabilizing factor in the midst of change.

Successful leaders interact with their customers, and encourage employees at all levels to do the same. This can be accomplished through scheduled customer visits to the organization for discussions, observations and feedback, and by sending representatives out to the customer's business. Once there, their job is to objectively observe exactly how specific products and services are being used and applied. They also interpret what problems occur and why, as well as each one's impact on various time factors.

This allows leaders to cross-pollinate ideas and concepts throughout the organization so that all involved have mutual goals and objectives, increasing the overall quality of the product and its value to the customer.

Additionally, employee exposure to their customers makes daily tasks and assignments more tangible. Employees are able to see how the product they produce is used. This increases empowerment and overall responsibility toward the customer.

Making It Fun

The concept of change and accompanying process of organizational transformation are stressful. Most leaders have learned that they can ease stress by making certain elements of the process "fun." This is not to say that leaders create a jovial and joking atmosphere, but that there is pleasure and enjoyment in accomplishing something together as a team and sharing interesting failures and mistakes in a non-critical atmosphere. It means keeping things light, celebrating the little successes, and using them to build on others to the accomplishment of mutual goals and objectives.

Change will throw many curves at an organization. It takes large doses of flexibility and participation to adapt to these trials. It also helps if leaders and employees lighten up at times where stress is at its highest, which helps to reduce the urge to take things far too seriously.

POINTS TO PONDER — SOMETHING TO THINK ABOUT

1. How active are you within your organizational unit? Are you continually out among your employees, being constantly visible?
2. How can you make the concept of change more "fun" in the sense of sharing successes and accomplishments? What other ideas can you think of?

TRAINING ACTIVITY — APPLICATION & ACTION PLAN

Within your organizational unit and level of responsibility, develop a program that allows you to formulate new ideas and concepts. Determine methods to quickly test and evaluate each one for their viability and feasibility.

Be creative. Analyze various factors and multiple techniques that will enable the unit to test concepts, ideas and strategies quickly, and ones that also allow them to "fail fast" and rapidly readjust. Apply lessons from past failures.

6

Handling Employees' Responses to Change

When faced with the prospect of change, the biggest fear employees will have is that of the unknown, especially if the change is perceived to threaten their jobs and personal economic security. This insecurity is often fed by rumors, as well as the impact that change has had on other companies, industries and the economy. Fears are heightened with the widespread dissemination of information through television, newspapers, the Internet and other media outlets.

The role of the leader is to be an agent and facilitator of change. This is underscored by their personal vision of the future. As agents and facilitators of change, leaders must understand that they will need to handle their employees' fears and apprehensions regarding future changes potentially affecting their jobs and personal security.

Individuals create their own "comfort zones," or established patterns and habits they are comfortable with. Change threatens these comfort zones and immediately places individuals in defensive modes as they attempt to protect their own personal "turfs."

IMPLICATIONS — WHAT THIS MEANS TO YOU

It is important for leaders to recognize employees' responses to change and show them that circumstances outside of their control make change inevitable. They must share and communicate information that employees can understand and react to in a way that gets them actively participating in the organizational transformation brought about by the forces of change. This means leaders must demonstrate to their employees that it is in their best interest to adapt if the organization is going to survive and prosper in the face of change.

STRATEGIES, TIPS & TECHNIQUES TO APPLY

There are a number of steps leaders can take to lessen their employee's apprehension and fear of change and facilitate smoother transitions.

Information

Leaders understand the need for open dialogue and discussion with their employees, and that this must be predicated on a complete sharing of available facts and figures with them so they can see for themselves what the organization is facing.

Employees' fears and apprehensions can be greatly reduced by sharing available information in order for them to understand the reasons for change, the factors that make it inevitable and the options available. This enables employees to see the challenges facing the organization and gives them opportunities to provide input as to possible alternatives and solutions.

When information is withheld, employees are suspicious of leadership's intentions and motivation. This undermines trust and confidence, and heightens fears and resistance.

Assurance

The idea of change and the transformation of an organization during times of change are stressful on all parties involved. Employees want their leaders' assurance that they will be treated fairly, that their ideas, feedback and input will be considered, and that they will be kept informed of the progress of changes and their potential impacts.

If there have been circumstances in the past where the organization has not treated their employees with consideration, sentiments of mistrust will be present that leaders must deal with. Building adequate levels of trust is a challenge for leaders, but enables them to lead their employees through periods of transformation.

Confidence

As leaders move their employees through an organizational transformation, they must make sure that they have built sufficient trust with them. Trust enables employees to have confidence in their leader's direction. This is also true for the upper levels of the organization. Employees must have confidence in all decisions being made during times of change.

Without adequate trust and confidence in their leadership, employees may trust the individual who is leading them at their specific level, but mistrust those higher up in the organization. This places the immediate leader in the precarious position of having to build employee's trust and confidence in senior leadership. Prior experiences with these senior leaders may foster more mistrust than trust. In these cases leaders on all levels must cooperate to instill trust and confidence in all employees.

Involvement

Leaders who respect their employees' intelligence and abilities lay the facts on the table and solicit their ideas, perspectives and input. Employee involvement in addressing issues like change bonds all together in the conquering of a common challenge. As the organization goes through a transformation, this cohesiveness is essential to ensure a smooth transition.

Involvement means gaining employee support and getting them actively working toward the development of a solution to everyone's benefit. When wise enough to ask, many leaders are astonished by the ideas and insight they receive from their employees. When the facts are placed before them and the choices spelled out, most employees will work together to achieve common goals and objectives. Most are actively involved because their future is at stake. There will be a certain percentage of employees who do not participate out of fear their contribution will be used against them. In these instances, leaders must inspire the rest of the group, hoping that positive peer pressure might influence more reluctant members to get involved.

Participation

The role of the leader is to lead employees through transformational change; the employee's job is to manage the change at their individual level. This means that in addition to their ideas, insights and feedback, employees must actively participate in implementing them on an individual level. When this active involvement is cultivated, and employees are informed and actively part of the development of the solutions, resistance and fear of change can be minimized. This is because leaders have empowered their employees both through ownership of ideas and the responsibility for seeing them successfully implemented. It is only when orders and directives are handed down without reason and rationale that employee resistance and fears increase.

Feedback

Leaders know how to close the loop by providing employees with active feedback regarding the results of their efforts to transform the organization. This continual feedback provides a supply of accurate information enabling employees to make informed decisions on how to successfully adapt their ideas to new variables and conditions.

POINTS TO PONDER — SOMETHING TO THINK ABOUT

1. What kinds of employee fears and apprehensions are you seeing in your department and organization?
2. What actions do you specifically take to resolve employee fears and apprehensions?

TRAINING ACTIVITY — APPLICATION & ACTION PLAN

Begin to hold frequent and regular discussions with your employees to share information with them regarding the forces of change that are impacting the organization.

1. Hold open discussions on how these changes are specifically challenging the organization and how it can handle them.
2. In your discussion, solicit additional input as to how these challenges are impacting specific employees. Ask for ideas, feedback and solutions.
3. As these discussions continue, begin to formulate plans for implementing positive changes within your department and organization, one step at a time.

7

Using Change to Increase Performance

The impact of change can often seem overwhelming to leaders, as most problems associated with it require the complete cooperation and participation of employees. This is especially true of problems occurring during the incremental phases comprising major changes, requiring countless decisions before effective solutions and methods can be implemented.

IMPLICATIONS — WHAT THIS MEANS TO YOU

A single event or person does not control change. Change is often brought about by a series of internal and external forces that impact all within the organization. The forces that bring about change are too dynamic for any single individual to oversee and direct. Consequently, for change to be managed and controlled effectively, the willing participation and input of an organization's entire workforce must be harnessed.

Change demands that all employees become actively involved, not only in the process of change itself, but also in the many decisions that change requires if a successful transformation is to occur.

STRATEGIES, TIPS & TECHNIQUES TO APPLY

Decision making and leadership is a dynamic process in the face of change. Rather than passively dealing with change, leaders must become proactive in their decision making, using the dynamics of change to increase performance and improve overall results.

The elements that enhance overall decision making in a dynamic atmosphere include:

Freely Empowered Employees

There is no set formula or pattern for implementing or dealing with change. As an organization transforms itself, change is implemented by countless daily decisions made at all levels of the organization, which are solely guided by the leader's vision. Unless employees, teams and workgroups are freely and fully empowered to make these decisions, a centralized decision making process remains in effect. This only works to hamper the organization's ability to readily adapt to change. Centralized decision making quickly bogs leaders down, greatly reducing their effectiveness and motivation.

Leaders must ensure their employees are free to make operational decisions on issues impacting their jobs and performance. Even reluctant employees will be swept into the waves of change, compelling them to be full, active participants in the process, regardless of their feelings or apprehensions.

Free-Flow of Information

The facilitation of effective decision making demands an open exchange of information. In the past, managers controlled information as a means of holding power and influence. In the face of change and transformation, all parties must be free to share all useful information and data so that more informed and lower-risk decisions can be consistently and expediently made.

A free-flow of information is not channeled into a single direction. It demands progression openly and in all directions, so that all parties are fully informed regarding the progress and impact of change at any given point in time. This gives the organization the ability to react quickly, and also allows it to readily adapt to changes on a needed basis.

Open Communication

Leaders must facilitate open channels of communication. Open communication encourages otherwise reluctant employees to report bad news or poor results free of fear of retaliation or punishment. If change is to be effectively managed, employees must feel free to openly communicate their feelings, observations, criticisms and findings with confidence that what they have to say will be fully respected and considered.

Encourage Experimentation

Change incorporates countless new ideas and concepts. Employees must be encouraged to take risks and try new methods and experiments. Not every idea will be successful or even feasible. Because of the pioneering nature of change, it is imperative employees understand they will be awarded the necessary freedom to experiment and tinker with new ideas, trial-and-error methods and creative concepts in order to isolate what works does and does not work.

The fact that many ideas might fail should be emphasized to help reduce frustration levels. In the midst of change transformation, failure is not as important as the lessons gained from it. Employees need to be encouraged to share their findings with others in the organization. The key is to test quickly and frequently in order to move the organization forward as expeditiously as possible.

Frequent Assessment

Leaders should hold frequent meetings with their employees to assess the progress of change within the organization. Their primary purpose is to share information and results based on the successes and failures of various ideas, trials and approaches.

Meetings should be used as a tool to tap the power of the group and provide realistic feedback and suggestions from astute observations. A successful meeting generates multiple employee perspectives and insights in order to disclose and detail what is working or not working within the organization.

Drive Down Decision Making

Leaders must drive decision making down deep within their organization. They must allow employees, teams and workgroups to make the daily tactical and operational decisions directly affecting their individual jobs.

Allowing members of the organization to generate decisions and solutions does not mean the leader shuns the responsibility of remaining actively involved in their decision making process. Rather, the decisions are guided by the leader's vision and direction, and many will necessitate his or her input. However, to get the most out of their employees on a consistent basis, leaders empower them to make group and individual decisions having a direct impact upon their individual performance.

Close the Decision Making Loop

Leaders must ensure all decision making loops are closed by closely monitoring the results of the collective decisions of their employees, teams and workgroups. Leaders must then share these findings with their employees so they can make any necessary adjustments, improvements or modifications based upon their feedback. Readjustment and the quest for improvement will naturally channel the process back to the starting point of the free-flow of information.

POINTS TO PONDER — SOMETHING TO THINK ABOUT

1. How freely do you allow information and communication to flow to your employees?
2. How involved are your employees in making tactical decisions that affect their unit, responsibilities and work?

TRAINING ACTIVITY – APPLICATION & ACTION PLAN

Based upon the decision making elements of this lesson, evaluate your own leadership efforts to create organizational change.

1. Review each of the following elements:
    - Freely empowered employees
    - Free-flow of information
    - Open communication
    - Encouragement of experimentation
    - Frequent assessment
    - Driving down decision making
    - Closing the decision making loop
2. Determine if you have created an effective decision making environment.
3. Identify areas of weakness.
4. Determine what actions need to be taken to make the decision making process more efficient and effective.

8

Facilitating Change

The facilitation of change is not the responsibility of any single individual, but is guided and directed by leadership on many different levels. Because change is dynamic, leadership must be equally so to keep pace with the opportunities and challenges it brings.

Leaders must understand change is not a destination but a process. The global economy does not allow leaders the luxury of resting on their laurels. Rather, it gives them the impetus to change and adapt on a frequent and regular basis. A failure to adapt opens the door to the forces of change overwhelming an organization.

IMPLICATIONS — WHAT THIS MEANS TO YOU

A "management mentality" in the face of change produces a specific outcome, which is essentially to ask, "The organization is changing—now what?"

Leaders on the other hand become the real and active facilitators of change. They understand the forces behind it and use its dynamics as a means to effectively and repeatedly transform their organization. Rather than fear the concept of change, leaders welcome the opportunities it affords them.

STRATEGIES, TIPS & TECHNIQUES TO APPLY

Facilitating change within any organization requires proactive participation from all of its leaders. In the dynamic atmosphere of change, leaders must be ever-present and visible. There are a number of proven leadership techniques one can employ to successfully facilitate change within their organization, including:

Promoting their Vision Daily

The importance of the leader's personal vision is a guiding and fundamental leadership principle. It is not sufficient for leaders to simply state their vision; they must actively promote and talk about it at every opportunity. It is necessary for leaders to continually remind employees of their direction as they guide them step-by-step through the processes, transitions, problems and successes en route to attaining their vision.

As changes occur within an organization, leaders must take advantage of every opportunity to spotlight events and people in order to showcase individual and group initiatives demonstrating progress toward the defined vision.

Leading by Personal Example

One of the most valuable resources available to a leader is time. Time is at a premium, and leaders must schedule carefully to achieve what is personally important to them. When employees see that their leaders are organized around the strategic priorities established to facilitate change, it communicates that they are in earnest about their personal initiatives.

As a general practice, leaders need to adjust their personal calendars to reflect the strategic priorities of facilitating change. This communicates that the leader is leading with action to back up their words, as they are focusing their time specifically upon the point of change.

Practicing Visible Leadership

Leaders cannot lead from behind a desk or office door. They must be present at the point of change to train, coach, cajole and comfort.

Leaders can only observe and learn when they are in the midst of their employees during the implementation of change. This is not a one-time event, but an ongoing exercise. This is why the efficient scheduling of time is critical if leaders want to be actively involved in the direct facilitation of change transformations.

Being a Compulsive Listener

Leaders have one primary responsibility: to go out and listen to their employees. It should not be done in a passive style of listening, but one where leaders actively engage their employees, learn from their frustrations, take action to clean up a particular stressful or unproductive situation, and enthusiastically encourage each one of them. The process of facilitating change requires that leaders make it an ongoing habit to actively listen and make necessary changes based upon what they specifically learn and observe.

Honoring Your Frontline Staff

Leaders understand that the point of change happens in the front lines of their organization. While it impacts the entire organization, the front lines are the apex of change. This is where its real impact is felt—and where leaders must directly focus their time, efforts and attention.

In this regard, leaders should be honoring their frontline employees. They accomplish this by celebrating all major and minor successes and learning from failures as they test new ideas and concepts.

Delegating

When leaders delegate they are not only freeing up valuable time, they are empowering and training others to perform key tasks. Proper delegation allows leaders to be more responsive to the needs of their organization because they can get out from under tasks demanding their time and hindering their ability to lead. The key to successful delegation is the maintenance of high standards for those the leader designates to perform the delegated work.

Managing Horizontally

When leaders manage horizontally, they are opening up communications and responsiveness at the front lines of their organization, and across multiple functions. This minimizes the delays of bureaucratic up and down communications and replaces it with faster frontline communications across functional boundaries. This allows leaders to test, try, modify, and act on ideas quickly, and facilitates change more rapidly at its apex and focal point.

Questioning Daily Progress

It is easy for leaders to mask a number of functions, items and agendas under the label of change. An effective leader constantly questions his or her progress on a daily basis and asks, "What exactly have I changed?"

Rather than measuring progress over time, leaders understand that facilitating change involves countless decisions and minor changes that produce organizational modifications, alterations or elimination of unproductive practices across many planes and avenues. They are more pragmatic about looking at specific daily changes to ensure that transformations are taking place throughout their organization.

Creating a Sense of Urgency

While the nature of change brings about its own sense of pressure, leaders must continually reinforce their personal sense of urgency to overcome all of the potentially paralyzing fears employees may experience due to change and its compelling nature. Every action and activity a leader undertakes must also be viewed as an unequivocal call for urgency in the pursuit of constant testing and improvement in subsequent change transformations throughout the organization.

POINTS TO PONDER — SOMETHING TO THINK ABOUT

1. Does your personal calendar reflect your strategic priorities?
2. How visible are you to your employees? How can you improve your visibility?

TRAINING ACTIVITY — APPLICATION & ACTION PLAN

1. Take a sheet of paper and list the following items in a column:
    - Promote vision daily
    - Lead by personal example
    - Practice visible leadership
    - Be a compulsive listener
    - Honor your frontline staff
    - Delegate
    - Manage horizontally
    - Question daily progress
    - Create a sense of urgency
2. Next to each, write down one or two activities or actions you can do on a daily basis to allow you to effectively facilitate change within your unit, department or organization.

About the Author

Timothy F. Bednarz, Ph.D. is CEO of the American Management Development Group, Inc. For over 20 years he has researched, designed and authored hundreds of learning and development programs used by Fortune 1000 companies.

He is also the author of *Great! What Makes Leaders Great. What They Did, How They Did It and What You Can Learn from It* (2011).

Speaking Availability

Timothy F. Bednarz, Ph.D. is available for speaking engagements for your next meeting or association event. He can be contacted at 800-654-4935 or by e-mail at timothy.bednarz@majorium.com.

Bulk Sales

Bulk sales of this book or any other titles available from Majorium Business Press. Inquiries can be directed to sales@majorium.com, or by phone at 800-6654-4935.

Quick Order Form

Fax orders: 715-342-1118. Send this form.

Telephone orders: Call 800-654-4935 toll-free. Have your credit card ready.

Email orders: sales@majorium.com

Postal orders: Majorium Business Press, 2025 Main Street, Stevens Point, WI 54481, USA.

Please send the following books:

____

____

____

____

Please send more FREE information on:

☐ Catalog ☐ Speaking/Seminars ☐ Mailing Lists ☐ Consulting

Name: ____________________________________

Address: __________________________________

City: ____________________ State: _____ Zip: _________

Telephone: ________________________________

Email address: ____________________________

Sales tax: Please add 5.5% for products shipped to Wisconsin addresses.

Shipping by air:

United States: $4.00 for first book and $2.00 for each additional product.

International: $9.00 for first book; $5.00 for each additional product (estimate).

Made in United States
Cleveland, OH
05 November 2026

47664315R00032